WHAT MAKES IT GO?

Written by Rod Barkman

CARS

Enslow PUBLISHING

Published in 2027 by Enslow Publishing, LLC
2544 Clinton Street
Buffalo, NY 14224

Written by: Rod Barkman
Edited by: Beth Latham
Designed by: Amelia Harris

Cataloging-in-Publication Data

Names: Barkman, Rod.
Title: Cars / Rod Barkman.
Description: Buffalo, NY : Enslow Publishing, 2027. | Series: What makes it go? | Includes glossary and index.
Identifiers: ISBN 9781978548213 (pbk.) | ISBN 9781978548220 (library bound) | ISBN 9781978548237 (ebook)
Subjects: LCSH: Automobiles--Juvenile literature.
Classification: LCC TL147.B375 2027 | DDC 629.222--dc23

Printed in China

CPSIA compliance information: Batch #QS27ENS: For further information contact Enslow Publishing LLC, New York, New York at 1-800-398-2504.

Please visit our website, www.enslowpublishing.com. For a free color catalog of all our high-quality books, call toll free 1-800-398-2504 or fax 1-877-980-4454.

Find us on

Image Credits

Images courtesy of Shutterstock.com, unless otherwise stated.

Cover and Recurring – Donglpix, Brandon Woyshni. 2–3 – Sanket27. 4–5 – Virrage Images, algre. 6–7 – GoodMan_Ekim, AstroStar. 8–9 – arda savasciogullari, Best Auto Photo, Just dance, Andrii Nesterov, Motorsport Photography F1. 10–11 – AvokadoStudio, Everyonephoto Studio, RYosha. 12–13 – Nordroden, Joe deSousa, CC0, via Wikimedia Commons. 14–15 – patruflo, asharkyu, VectorMine. 16–17 – Toa55, Quality Stock Arts. 18–19 – KOTOIMAGES, Andriy Baidak. 20–21 – New Africa, BongkarnGraphic, vpvhunter. 22–23 – Gorodenkoff, Vietnam Stock Images.

CONTENTS

WORDS THAT LOOK LIKE THIS CAN BE FOUND IN THE GLOSSARY ON PAGE 24.

WHAT IS A CAR?

Cars are vehicles that drive on land. They usually have four wheels. They are powered by engines, which either burn fuel or run on electricity. Cars have seats for the driver and some passengers.

What kinds of cars have you traveled in?

The person who controls the car is called the driver. Everyone else in the car is called a passenger. There are many different parts to a car.

CARS IN EVERYDAY LIFE

Cars are mostly used to move people from one place to another. People use cars to go to work, school, and other places. Some people go on long car rides called road trips to travel far away.

Cars are also used in sports, such as this rally car.

Cars are also important for jobs all around the world, such as taxi drivers and delivery drivers. People who work in some emergency services, such as police officers, also use cars to do their jobs.

TYPES OF CARS

There are all sorts of different cars. Have you seen any of these cars in real life?

SUVs are big and look like a cross between a car and a truck.

Hatchbacks are medium-sized cars. The rear part opens by swinging upward.

A limousine is a type of long car. It can cost a lot of money to be driven around in a limousine!

A race car can look very different from an everyday car. It is made to go extremely fast around a racetrack.

A convertible is a car that has a roof that folds down.

ON THE INSIDE

The driver turns the car using a steering wheel. The dashboard shows the driver information, such as how fast the car is going and how much fuel is left. There are levers for blinkers and headlights.

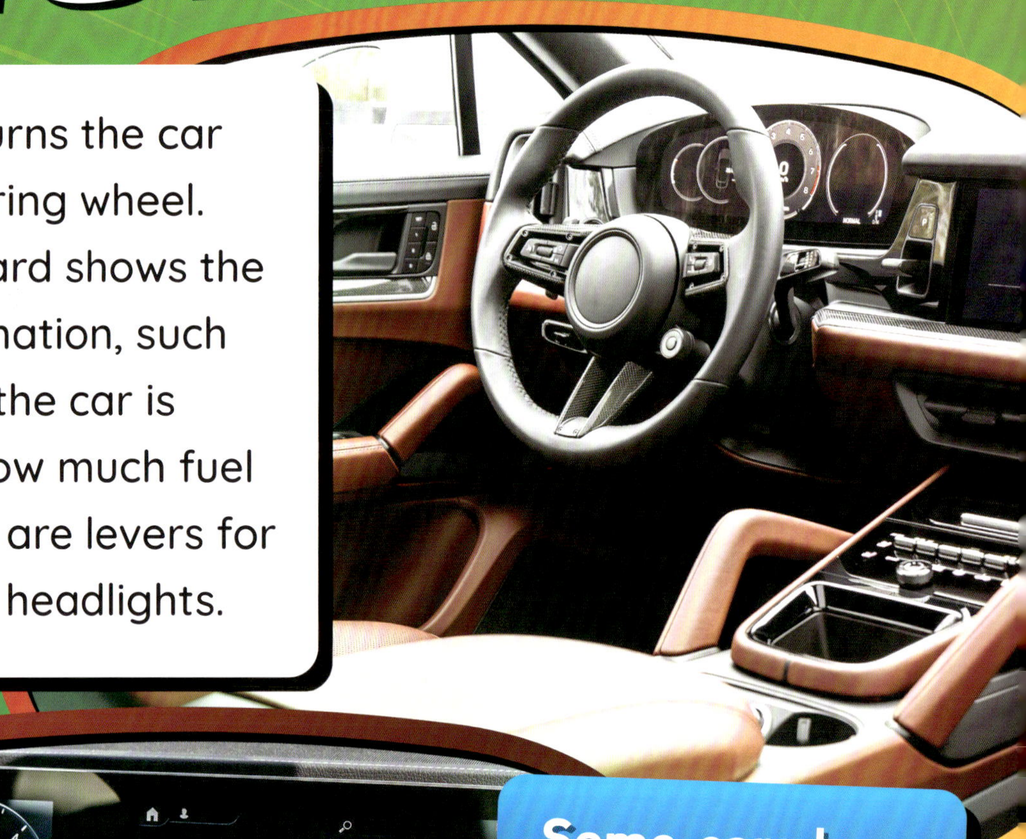

Some cars have touchscreens for certain controls.

There are also pedals by the driver's feet. The brake pedal is usually on the left or in the middle. It stops the car. The pedal on the right is the accelerator. It controls how fast the car goes.

Some cars have a third pedal called the clutch, which helps control the engine.

HISTORY

It is thought that one of the first automobiles, or cars, was invented in France in the 1700s. It had three wheels, and the engine was powered by steam. It was slow and could not run for long.

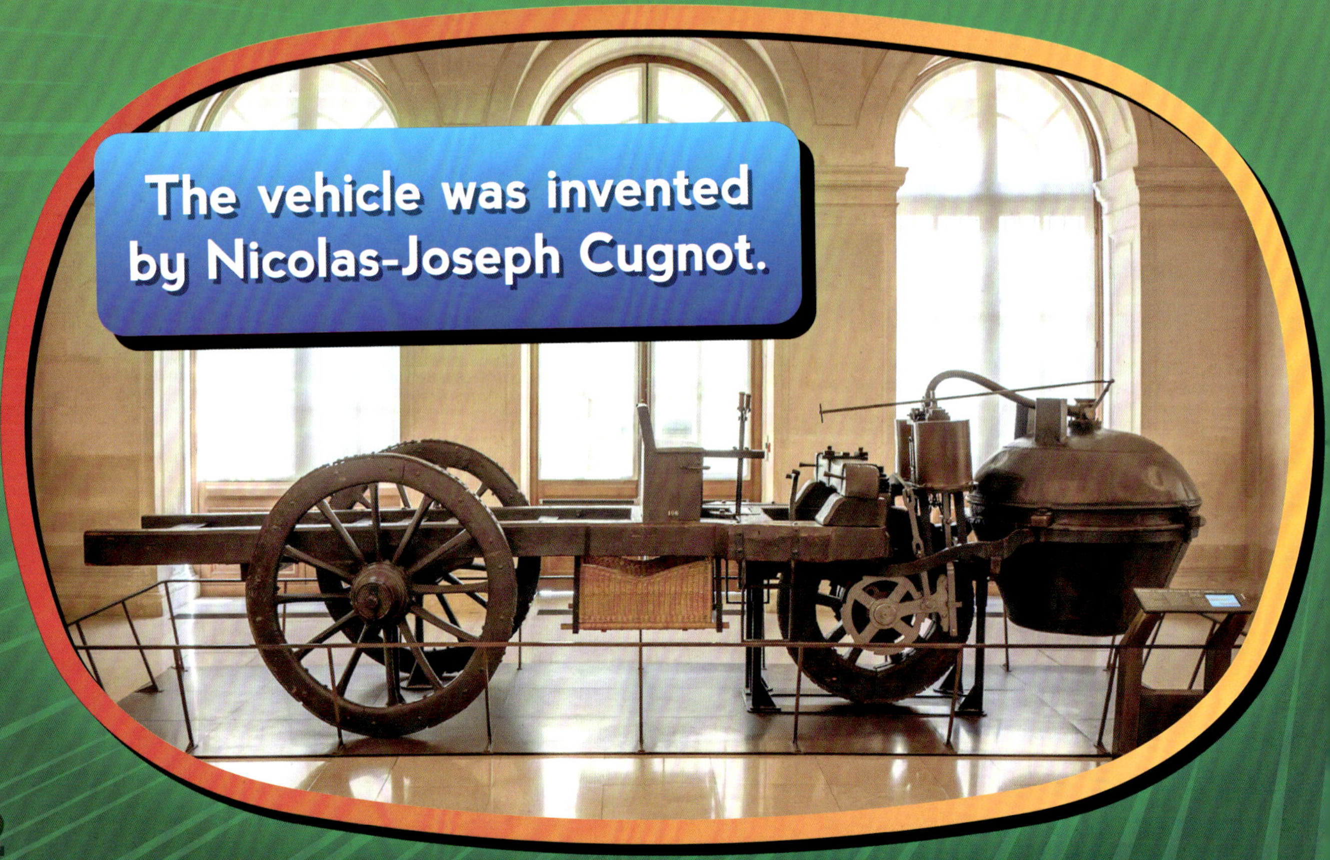

The vehicle was invented by Nicolas-Joseph Cugnot.

In the early 1900s, the Ford Model T was invented. This type of car was sturdier and cheaper than other cars, which meant lots of people could buy it.

THE FORD MODEL T WAS MADE ON AN ASSEMBLY LINE, WHICH MEANT EACH CAR COULD BE PUT TOGETHER QUICKLY.

HOW DO ENGINES WORK?

Many cars have combustion engines. These engines burn fuel to create small explosions, which move pistons up and down. The moving pistons turn a rod called a crankshaft. This turns the wheels of the car.

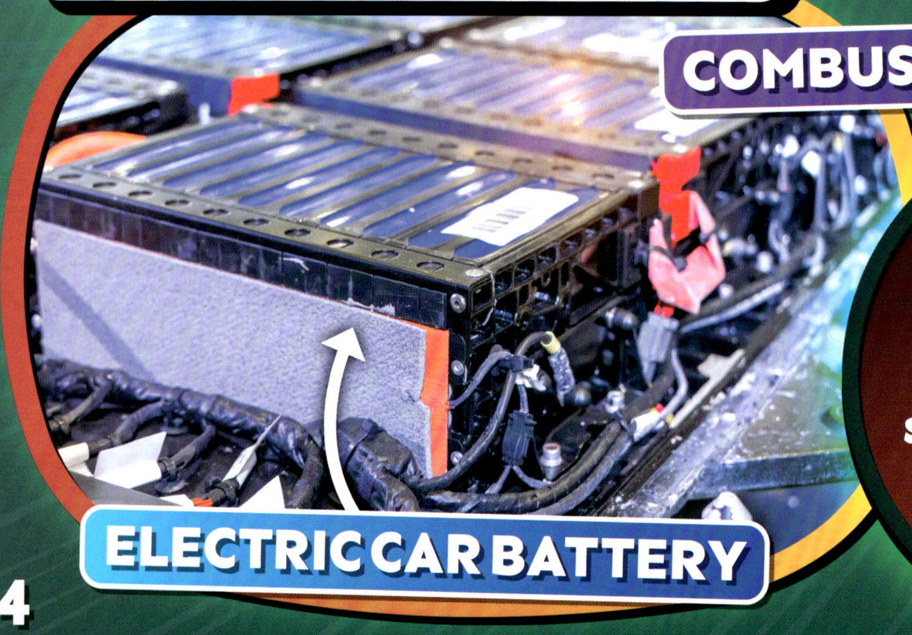

ELECTRIC CAR ENGINES ARE DIFFERENT. THERE IS A BATTERY THAT SPINS A ROTOR, AND THIS TURNS THE WHEELS.

A combustion engine has four stages, or strokes.

1. Fuel comes in from the top as the piston moves down.

2. The piston moves up, squeezing the air and fuel.

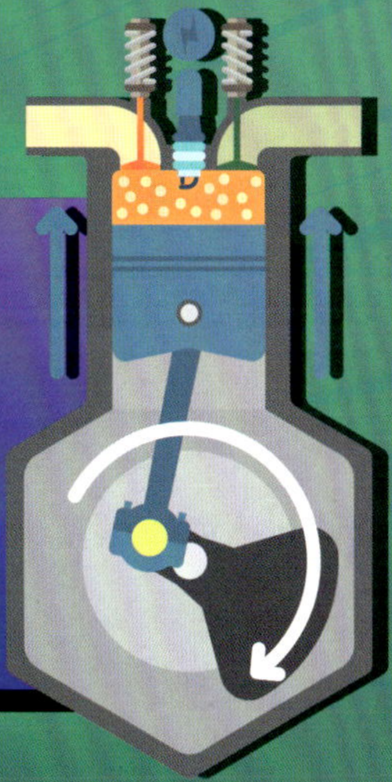

3. A spark burns the fuel, and the explosion knocks the piston down.

4. The piston bounces back up, pushing the burned gases out of the top.

HOW DO CARS MOVE?

The engine turns the crankshaft, which is connected to gears of different sizes. The gears are linked to something called a driveshaft, which is a kind of long stick. The driveshaft spins when the engine runs.

The other end of the driveshaft is attached to more gears. As these gears turn, they spin a long rod called an axle. On each end of the axle is a car wheel.

SCIENCE OF CARS

When a car moves forward, it pushes against the air. This slows the car down, which is called drag. However, a more smoothly shaped car moves through air easier. This means there is less drag and the car goes faster.

Racing cars have a slim, smooth shape so there is less drag.

Racing cars have special parts that force air to press down on the car. This is called downforce. Downforce helps keep the car on the road so the driver can go around corners quickly.

The front splitter pushes air over and under the car in ways that create downforce.

SAFETY

Cars are full of things to keep people safe. When a car crashes, airbags automatically come out of either the steering wheel or the dashboard. These act as cushions to protect people inside the car.

Seatbelts were one of the earliest safety inventions in a car.

A crumple zone is an area of a car that is made to be easily crushed, such as the front of the car. Some of the force of a crash is absorbed by the crumple zone.

THE FUTURE

Some fuels can be harmful to the planet, such as gasoline or diesel. Electric cars can be better for the planet, as long as the electricity comes from renewable energy sources. In the future, more cars will be electric.

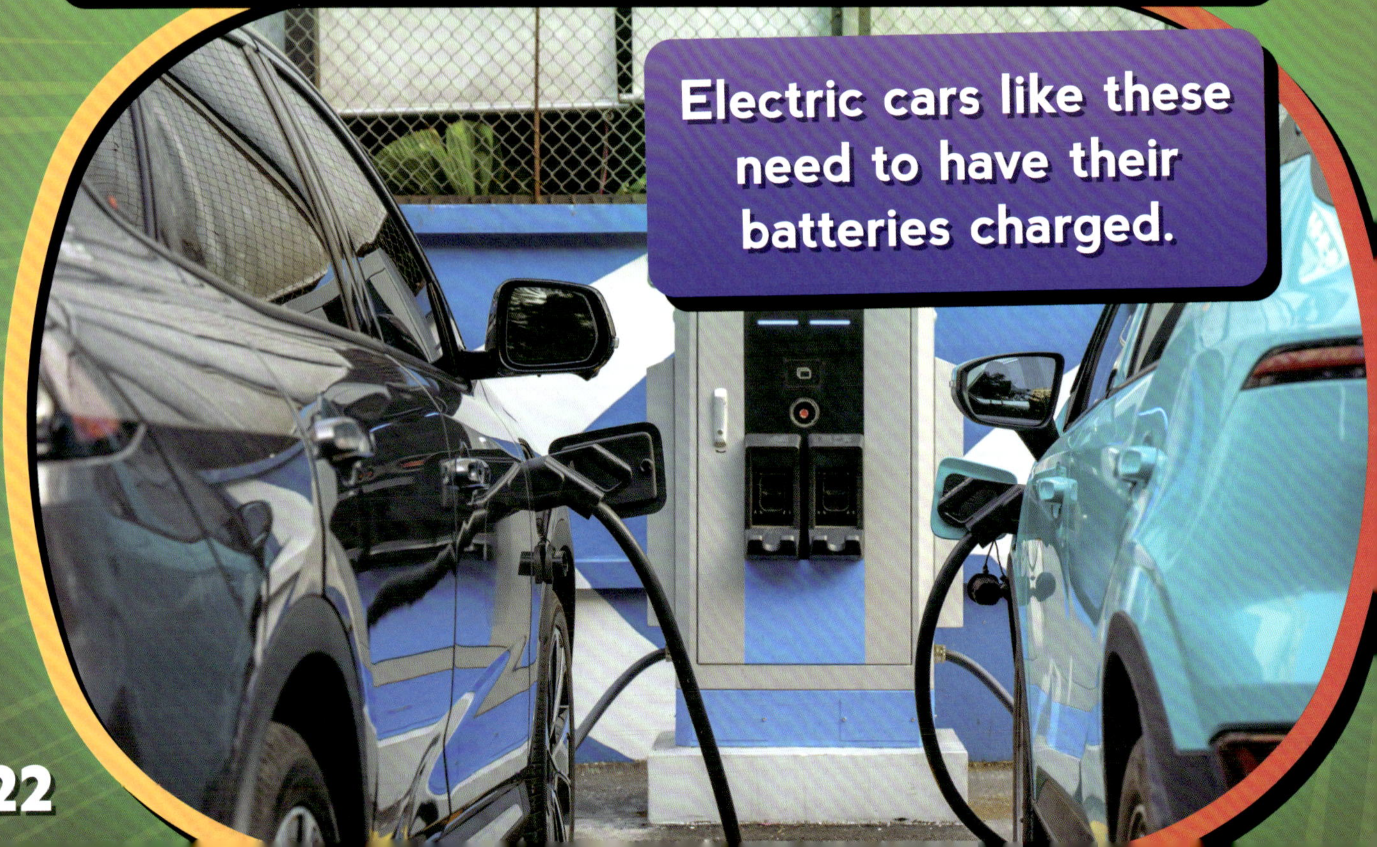

Electric cars like these need to have their batteries charged.

Self-driving cars use cameras, radar, and sensors to see what is around them. Right now, these cars need help from human drivers. In the future, people might be driven around by fully self-driving cars.

Now that you know all about cars, what kind of car would you like to see in the future?

GLOSSARY

absorbed to have taken in or soaked up

blinkers small flashing lights on the side of a vehicle that can be turned on to show other drivers which way the vehicle is about to go when it is turning

fuel something that can be used to power something else

gases things that are like air, which fill any space available

gears small wheels that fit together inside a machine

pistons small, solid parts of a machine that move up and down

radar a way of finding where something is by sending out radio waves, which are bounced back

renewable energy power made from sources that do not run out, such as wind or energy from the sun

rotor a part of a machine that rotates or spins, especially in vehicles

INDEX